DATE DUE

APR 1 3 2009		
MAY 0 5 2009		

DWIGHT D. EISENHOWER

ENCYCLOPEDIA
of PRESIDENTS

Dwight D. Eisenhower

Thirty-Fourth President of the United States

By Jim Hargrove

Consultant: Charles Abele, Ph.D.
Social Studies Instructor
Chicago Public School System

℗ CHILDRENS PRESS ®
CHICAGO

Eisenhower and his wife, Mamie, on his seventy-second birthday, October 14, 1962

Library of Congress Cataloging-in-Publication Data

Hargrove, Jim.
    Dwight D. Eisenhower.

    (Encyclopedia of presidents)
    Includes index.
    1. Eisenhower, Dwight D. (Dwight David), 1890-1969—
Juvenile literature.   2.   Presidents—United States—
Biography—Juvenile literature.   3.   Generals—United
States—Biography—Juvenile literature.   4.   United
States. Army—Biography—Juvenile literature.   I.   Title.
II.   Series.
E836.H27   1987   973.921′092′4 [B]   86-29918
ISBN 0-516-01389-0

Childrens Press, Chicago
Copyright ©1987 by Regensteiner Publishing Enterprises, Inc.
All rights reserved. Published simultaneously in Canada.
Printed in the United States of America.

        13 14 15 16 17 18 19 20 R 02 01 00 99

Picture Acknowledgments

AP/Wide World—28, 52, 60, 67, 71, 76, 77, 78,
79, 80, 81, 82, 83

Courtesy Dwight D. Eisenhower Library—6, 9,
11, 13, 17, 26, 29, 32, 39, 40, 42, 43, 44, 46, 48,
57, 61, 62 (bottom), 68, 85, 88

Eisenhower Museum, Abilene, Kansas—18, 22,
25, 27, 30

Historical Pictures Service—41, 69, 73

Kansas State Historical Society, Topeka,
Kansas—21, 31

Library of Congress—15, 23, 38, 55, 84, 86, 89

United Press International—4, 5, 8, 10, 45, 47,
51, 53, 54 (2 photos), 56, 58, 62 (top), 63 (2
photos), 64, 66, 75

Courtesy U.S. Department of the Army—16, 34,
35, 37

U.S. Bureau of Printing and Engraving—2

Cover design and illustration by
Steven Gaston Dobson

Eisenhower in 1957 delivering his inaugural address after taking the oath of office for his second term. Seated at left are Chief Justice Earl Warren and former President Herbert Hoover; at right is Vice-President Richard Nixon.

Table of Contents

Flying Fortresses of the U.S. Eighth Air Force on their way to bomb targets
in Nazi Germany, March 26, 1944

Chapter 1

D-Day

In the early days of June 1944, thousands of ships were being loaded with soldiers, weapons, and supplies in every port along the southern coast of England. General Dwight Eisenhower was there, too, watching ships and soldiers prepare for the largest military invasion in history. As Supreme Commander of Allied Forces in Europe, Eisenhower was in charge of the entire attack.

In France, just across the English Channel, German soldiers ruled the land. Like most of the other nations of Europe, France had been conquered by Germany during the early years of World War II. Under the cruel leadership of Adolf Hitler, German troops had already killed millions of European and Asian soldiers trying to defend their homelands. Millions more civilians, European Jews, gypsies, and enemies of the Nazi empire, already had been murdered in German concentration camps.

Nations not conquered by the Nazi war machine, principally the United States, England, Russia, and Canada, organized their armies to attack the German soldiers in Europe. These armies were called the Allied forces. Near the end of 1943, the American general Dwight Eisenhower was put in charge of all the armies prepared to fight Adolf Hitler's troops in Western Europe.

A British landing barge off the shore of Tripoli in North Africa

American and British airplanes had been bombing German military targets for some time, but it was impossible to liberate Europe without an invasion on land. Eisenhower's orders were as easy to understand as they were difficult to carry out. "You will enter the continent of Europe," he was told by the governments of the Allied nations, and "undertake operations aimed at the heart of Germany and the destruction of her armed forces." So that the Germans would not be prepared for the attack, the exact date of the invasion was kept a secret. It was simply referred to as D-Day. The invasion was code-named "Operation Overlord."

British Prime Minister Winston Churchill (center) and General Eisenhower inspect equipment in Newbury, England.

For more than a year, Eisenhower had been working with American president Franklin Roosevelt, with British prime minister Winston Churchill, and with many military leaders to plan the enormous invasion. As early as 1942, the Allied nations began stockpiling weapons in England for the attack. Millions of tons of weapons and equipment were brought to England in preparation for Operation Overlord. In the month of June 1944 alone, 1,900,000 tons of supplies were brought to England by Allied forces. As D-Day approached, about 5,000 Allied ships and 1,200 airplanes were ready for the attack. Although he had many aides to help him, Dwight Eisenhower was ultimately responsible for every soldier and every piece of equipment gathered for the invasion.

On an inspection tour of England, Ike tells the troops, "If you men can fight as well as you are doing this training, God help the Nazis."

For all his power, Eisenhower was a modest man. He enjoyed the fact that many soldiers called him by his nickname, Ike. "When they called me Ike," he once said, "I knew that everything was going well." Soldiers liked Ike not only because he was a great leader, but also because he did not believe in many of the unnecessary routines that were often part of their lives.

"He is noted for his great energy and hatred of routine office work," a Nazi officer told other German soldiers. "Eisenhower enjoys the greatest popularity with Roosevelt and Churchill." The officer also pointed out that Ike was skilled at working with other soldiers, "whom he manages to inspire to supreme efforts through kind understanding and easy discipline."

General Charles de Gaulle of France visits Ike in makeshift headquarters.

Although he made those around him feel that he was easygoing and relaxed, Eisenhower felt the pressure of planning the details of Operation Overlord. "I seem to live on a network of high tension wires," he wrote to his wife, Mamie, a week before the invasion.

The exact date of D-Day was one of the most closely guarded secrets of World War II. Conditions had to be just right for the difficult invasion of Europe. The tide had to be low, so that underwater fences the Germans had built along the coast of France could be found and destroyed. The night before D-Day, moonlight was needed so that soldiers could drop by parachute into the French countryside, behind the Nazis' shore defenses. And the precise time of the attack would have to be early morning, so that ships could approach under cover of darkness and attack at the first light of dawn.

For a year or so, Allied commanders had planned for Operation Overlord to begin in May of 1944. But for a number of reasons—especially that many ships had to be brought from the Mediterranean Sea to the English Channel—the invasion was delayed for a month. By the earliest days of June, however, it was clear to everyone, including the Germans, that the Allies were ready to invade France. But precisely where, and exactly when, was kept a secret.

On June 2, 1944, just days before D-Day, Eisenhower moved his headquarters from London to a large house near the English city of Portsmouth, where he could be closer to the ships preparing for the invasion. Although there was a comfortable home for his use, he spent much of his time in a tent set up nearby, where he could be closer to the other soldiers. There he made the last-minute plans for D-Day.

Although many of the soldiers around him were unaware of the secret date for the invasion of France, Ike knew that it was June 5. The actual invasion was set to begin on the evening of June 4, when ships would leave dozens of English ports and sail slowly toward France. At the same time, an army of paratroopers would drop from planes into the French countryside.

As he stood outside his tent near Portsmouth on the evening of June 3, Ike knew that trouble was brewing. He had made the most careful of plans for the invasion. Soldiers, ships, airplanes, tanks, trucks, jeeps, guns, ammunition, landing craft, bombs, food, medical supplies, communications equipment, spare parts, and even huge structures to make artificial harbors were all at the ready. Only one thing could not be planned: the weather.

England, March 1944: Eisenhower, Winston Churchill, and General Omar Bradley engage in a bit of target practice.

Outside Ike's tent in southern England, the wind was increasing and the sky was darkening. "The weather in this country is practically unpredictable," he complained, and he was soon proved correct. Captain J. M. Stagg, Ike's chief weather forecaster, said that the weather on June 5 would be stormy. Conditions were so uncertain, Stagg reported, that the weather was impossible to predict more than twenty-four hours in advance.

Even though it was only the evening of June 3, Eisenhower knew that he had to make a decision soon. Ships of the United States Navy, carrying the army of General Omar Bradley, were at anchor in the Atlantic, awaiting word to steam toward France. Since they had farther to travel than the other Allied ships and planes in England, word to begin or wait would have to be given to them quickly. Eisenhower decided to start the ships, but to alert them for a possible cancellation the next morning.

At 4:30 on the morning of June 4, well before dawn, Ike met with his assistants and weather forecaster Stagg. Stagg reported that the seas would be calmer than expected, but that heavy clouds would make airplane flight almost impossible. Knowing that the landing troops would need cover from airplanes overhead, Ike and the other military commanders decided to delay the attack for twenty-four hours. The new date for D-Day was June 6.

On the evening of June 4, Eisenhower again met with his advisers and listened intently to the new weather report. By 9:30, Stagg had revised his forecast. There would be a break in the storm the next day, he said. It was hard to believe the report. Outside, the rain was falling heavily and the wind was howling.

Many of Eisenhower's top advisers thought it was impossible to begin an attack in such terrible weather. Nevertheless, at 9:45 that evening Eisenhower said, "I am quite positive that the order must be given." In minutes, his decision was passed along to the other commanders awaiting word of the invasion. More than five thousand ships began steaming toward France.

When he awoke at 3:30 A.M. on the morning of June 5, sheets of rain were driven sideways by a fierce wind. It looked as if he had made a terrible mistake. At a meeting with other military leaders before dawn, Eisenhower tried to decide whether to call off the invasion yet again. The great fleet of Allied ships was already entering the English Channel. Soon they would be spotted by German soldiers. The decision had to be made. But even as the soldiers talked, the rain began to lessen.

Ike talking to U.S. paratroopers before their invasion of France

"O.K.," Eisenhower said, "let's go." As soon as he gave that command, the other soldiers with him cheered and then left to go to their posts. Suddenly Eisenhower was alone. After more than a year of planning, there was now little more that he could do.

On the evening of June 5, the ships approached their landing sites along the coast of France. In England, huge fleets of planes were given final checks and sent into the air to bomb German fortifications and to drop paratroopers onto French soil. Ike and some other soldiers drove to the English city of Newbury, where the 101st Airborne Division was preparing to take off for France. Among the troops, Ike watched the soldiers, whose faces were painted black to make them more difficult to see in the night.

In Le Havre, France, Ike talks to soldiers going to a reinforcement camp.

"Now stop worrying," one of the men told Eisenhower. "We'll take care of this for you, General." The soldier was right. By the following morning, the first troops landed on the beaches of France. Nazi soldiers, expecting the invasion elsewhere, were taken by surprise. For the first time since the start of the war, armies from free nations had arrived in Western Europe. By the end of D-Day, 132,000 Allied troops and 23,000 paratroopers had landed in France. As the days and weeks went by, they continued to come. By the first week of July, more than a million Allied soldiers had landed in France. There they were joined by thousands of soldiers from the French underground who were ready to fight the hated Nazis.

Ike and General George Patton (second from right) examine a German dugout encampment.

Operation Overlord was so successful that the Allied troops under Ike's command accomplished their mission in less than a year. By April of 1945, Nazi soldiers had retreated all the way to Germany, where they were soon destroyed or captured by Allied forces. What was left of the Nazi government surrendered in May.

Eisenhower's brilliant efforts in World War II made him a hero throughout much of the world. More than anything else, his fame as a soldier enabled him to become, some years later, the president of the United States. Operation Overlord was the largest invasion in world history, and the greatest achievement of Ike's long military career. It was not, however, his first taste of a military attack, real or imagined. That came much earlier.

The Eisenhowers in front of their house on Fourth Street in Abilene, Kansas.
Standing, left to right, are Milton, Ike, and Earl. Seated are parents
David and Ida. The dog is Flip.

Chapter 2

"Sweet Abilene"

During morning recess in the spring of 1898, many of the boys from Lincoln elementary school suddenly ran away from the schoolyard. One of the children was seven-year-old Dwight Eisenhower, already called "Little Ike" by his schoolmates and neighbors. (His older brother Edgar was known as "Big Ike.") The boys from Lincoln school had decided to play hooky because an alarming rumor had spread through their classrooms.

A few of the boys said—and now every one of them believed—that a Spanish "airship" had been spotted over downtown Abilene, Kansas, their hometown. All the boys soon decided that it was carrying soldiers and bombs ready to attack from the air.

Rumors are often curious, but today this story seems particularly so. After all, the first automobile was not seen in Abilene until well into the twentieth century. The Wright brothers would not fly the world's first powered airplane until late in 1903, more than five years after the supposed sighting of the Spanish airship.

Little Ike and his schoolmates, none of whom had even heard of an automobile or an airplane, rushed uptown. Each boy hoped to be the first to catch a glimpse of the dreaded—but terribly exciting—Spanish airship.

At the time, the United States was fighting a war with Spain around the island of Cuba. In February of 1898, the U.S. battleship *Maine* blew up and sank in a Cuban harbor, killing hundreds of sailors. Although no one knew for certain how the ship was destroyed, many Americans assumed that the Spanish were responsible. "Remember the *Maine*" soon became the battle cry for the soldiers who fought in the Spanish-American War, as well as for the schoolchildren of Abilene, Kansas.

The young students who raced uptown, Little Ike in their midst, had heard reports that the Spanish were using huge balloons, filled with hot air, to carry troops and weapons. Now one of the airships, as the balloons were called, was being used to attack Abilene! Relief and disappointment must have come at the same time when the boys spotted not an airship, but a large box kite that was being flown high above the town. The kite carried a printed advertisement for straw hats sold by a local store.

Although the town was a quiet place during the years Ike attended school, it had not always been that way. Just a few decades earlier, the Kansas town was one of the wildest places in the American West. Then, Abilene marked the western end of the Kansas-Pacific Railroad. Cowboys driving huge herds of cattle traveled over the Chisholm Trail through Texas, Oklahoma, and southern Kansas to the Abilene railroad station. There they sold their herds to cattle buyers who eventually loaded the animals onto railroad cars for the final journey eastward.

For the cowboys, Abilene was the end of a long, dirty, exhausting journey. As they came into town, many sang

Abilene in the horse-and-buggy days

and shouted a song that went "Abilene, sweet Abilene, prettiest town I've ever seen." Then they headed straight for one of the many saloons, where they sometimes drank too much whiskey and staggered onto the dirt street with six-shooters blazing. By 1870, Abilene was known as one of the most lawless cities in America.

In 1871, the famous frontiersman Wild Bill Hickok was hired as marshall in the hope that he could bring some peace to the riotous town. For a few months he restored some degree of order, but he soon left to join Buffalo Bill Cody's Wild West Show, which was touring cities in the eastern United States. Abilene gradually grew into a peaceful Kansas town as the railroad built tracks farther west, and it was no longer the end of the road. When cowboys and cattle buyers no longer came to town, many saloon keepers, dance hall girls, gamblers, and outlaws soon headed west with the railroad.

The first known photo of Dwight David Eisenhower, taken in Abilene in 1893 when he was three years old. Ike is at the bottom right. Behind him is Edgar. Arthur is holding Roy.

Not much later, in the spring of 1891, the family of David and Ida Eisenhower, Ike's parents, moved from their former home in Texas to Abilene. At the time, Ike was only a few months old. David and Ida were no strangers to the flat prairielands of Kansas. Just a few years earlier, before Ike was born, they had lived in the town of Hope, Kansas, where David ran a general store. One year a drought and an invasion of grasshoppers destroyed many of the crops in the area. Farmers were suddenly unable to pay the bills they owed Ike's father, and he soon went broke, unable to pay his own bills. The family then moved to Texas, where David worked in a creamery to pay off his bills. Dwight D. Eisenhower, the third of seven sons (one died as a baby), was born in Denison, Texas, on October 14, 1890.

Ike, Edgar, Earl, Roy, and Arthur Eisenhower in front of their Second Street house

During his earliest years, Ike and his brothers lived in a tiny house on Second Street in Abilene. Even though open land stretched out for hundreds of miles in every direction, many of the homes in Abilene were built on tiny lots. Dwight Eisenhower described the lot of his boyhood home with these words: "Our Second Street home was tiny. The front yard was a patch. The back yard, with wooden fences on each side and a coal and wood shed not far from the back of the house, was large enough to swing a cat in, if it were a small one."

A few months before his fifth birthday, Ike went on a horse-and-buggy trip with his Aunt Minnie to Topeka, Kansas, where many of his mother's relatives lived. In the years to come, Ike became a great general and a beloved president, but it was in the town of Topeka, Kansas, that the four-year-old boy fought his first great battle.

As he was exploring the backyard of his aunt's home, he noticed a pair of geese. As Ike was going closer to investigate, the male goose, or gander, decided that he had seen enough of the youngster. With terrible hissing and honking sounds and a violent flapping of the wings, the gander charged toward the boy, pushing him toward the back door of the house with his beak. In tears, the boy fled into the safety of the house.

"Thus," Ike wrote years later, "the war began." Every time the four-year-old ventured into the backyard, the gander made a fierce charge. And every time the gander attacked, Ike retreated in tears. Soon he was afraid to venture far beyond the back of the house.

Ike's Uncle Luther finally came to the rescue. Cutting off some of the bristles of an old broom to give it the proper firmness, Luther showed the boy how to swing it. Ike cautiously took the broom and advanced deeper into the yard. As expected, the gander soon made its noisy attack, but this time the boy was ready. Swinging the broom with all his might, he whacked the bird right on its tail. The four-year-old did no real harm, but the gander was so shocked that it returned to its corner of the yard, defeated. From that point on, Ike saw that the proper way to deal with an enemy was from a position of strength.

Back in Abilene, young Dwight entered the first grade at Lincoln School in the fall of 1896. Throughout his school years, he was an above-average student, although not exceptional. In those days, schoolwork could be quite boring. Often it involved memorizing long passages from books and then reciting them aloud.

Ike (in front)
on a campout
with his buddies

In his adult years, Eisenhower explained that much of his education came from home. Both his parents were very religious, and it was a custom for Ike and his brothers to read passages from the Bible aloud to the family. Each brother took a turn reading until he made a mistake. At that point, the privilege passed on to the next brother. In this way, all the Eisenhower brothers learned to read clearly and accurately.

In 1898, the same year that the Spanish airship was widely reported but never seen, the Eisenhower family moved into a larger house, purchased from a relative, on Fourth Street. Now the two parents and six brothers in the Eisenhower family finally had a little more room. It wasn't that much room, though. President Eisenhower said, years later, that one of his offices in Washington was larger than either of his boyhood homes.

Left to right: Arthur, Edgar, Ike, Roy, Earl, and Milton

More importantly, however, the new home had a yard large enough for planting vegetables. Ike's father gave each brother a plot of land to use as a garden. And each brother was allowed to sell the vegetables he grew for pocket money. When crops were good, new baseballs and mitts were plentiful in the Eisenhower household.

Unfortunately, there was no lack of chores around the house. At the time, American girls traditionally did almost all of the housework, but there was a distinct lack of daughters in the Eisenhower family. The brothers had to pitch in washing dishes, doing the laundry, and even cooking, a skill Ike developed quite early. Throughout his life, even in army mess tents, people often looked forward to meals prepared by Ike.

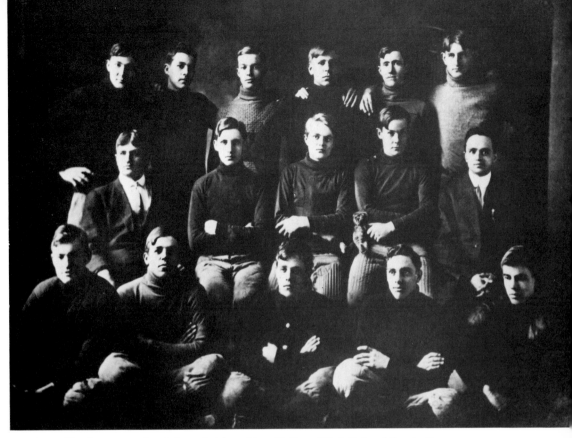

Ike (top row, third from left) and his Abilene High School football team

Although he preferred playing sports like baseball and football to classroom study, Eisenhower moved on to Garfield Junior High School on the north side of town, and then to Abilene High School in 1904. In a brand new building that was the pride of every student, the fourteen-year-old boy found new subjects to study. Although an infection brought about by a slight cut on his knee caused a serious illness that required him to repeat his freshman year, teachers at the school soon discovered that Ike had unusual skill in the branch of mathematics called geometry. In a fascinating experiment, the teachers asked him to try to study geometry without a textbook. They wanted Ike to discover the answer to every problem without any help at all! Much of the time, he was able to do it.

The Eisenhowers in 1902. Back row: Dwight, Edgar, Earl, Arthur, and Roy.
Front: David, Milton, and Ida

Ike also developed a stronger interest in reading. For
some time, he had been fascinated by ancient battles
fought by the Greeks and Romans. He read detailed stories
of the old wars and borrowed many books about them. At
one point, his mother, who hated war and felt it was usual-
ly avoidable, took the books away from him and locked
them in a closet. But he found the key and read them any-
way, whenever she wasn't looking.

Despite his new interest in reading and geometry, Ike's
greatest love throughout high school was sports. Whenever
he was not working at odd jobs to earn money, he enjoyed
playing baseball and football. At times, he even played

Ike's high school yearbook picture. The caption reads: "Little Ike," now a couple of inches taller than "Big Ike," is our best historian and mathematician. President of Athletic Association, '09; Football, '07, '08; Baseball '08, '09.

hooky from school so that he could go to a downtown office where telegraph operator Cecil Brooks announced the inning-by-inning scores for important big league baseball games. (In 1909, the same year that Ike graduated from high school, an Italian scientist named Guglielmo Marconi won the Nobel Prize for his pioneering work in the field of radio engineering. But the first radio station in America was not established until eleven years later.)

Two hundred Abilene children entered first grade along with Ike. Of those, only thirty-one graduated from high school. Ike was one of the proud graduates in 1909. With high school over, a great new adventure was beginning.

Ike was a hometown hero whenever he came home from West Point on vacation.
Here he is in Abilene Park in 1915 with his friend Jake Kruger.

The Belle Springs Creamery in Abilene, 1908

Chapter 3

A Soldier Out of Battle

On the morning of June 14, 1911, twenty-year-old Dwight Eisenhower arrived at the West Point station on a train that followed the Hudson River in New York State. Carrying his bags, he walked up a long hill toward the buildings of the United States Military Academy at West Point. At the Point, as the academy was often called, students were trained to become officers in the U.S. Army. As Ike was about to discover, life at the Point was considerably different than at a normal college.

The road from Abilene High School to West Point took two years for Ike to travel. After graduating from the Abilene school, he worked at various jobs in Kansas trying to earn money to help his brother Edgar pay for his expenses at the University of Michigan. Then, at the suggestion of his friend Everett Hazlett, he applied to become a student at the U.S. Naval Academy at Annapolis, Maryland. He was deeply disappointed when he discovered that, at the age of twenty, he was already too old to enter the Naval Academy. But with the help of a U.S. senator, he managed to get accepted at West Point.

Opposite page: Ike as a West Point cadet

Members of the Army football squad. Ike is fourth from the left.

From his very first day, he discovered that life at the Point was going to be difficult. As soon as he arrived, the other students, called cadets, began barking out orders at him. They told him to run, not walk, this way and that way, to keep his shoulders straight, to keep looking up, not down, and so on. As he began his studies, he discovered that instructors and army officers were just as strict as the upperclass cadets, demanding that everything be done in a very particular way. To a boy accustomed to life in a quiet Kansas town, it was quite a shock.

As a student at West Point, Ike's grades were just barely above average. As a football player for the famous West Point Army team, however, he did show outstanding talent. Many sportswriters believed that he would become an All-American, until a knee injury ended his career during his second year.

West Point lettermen of 1915. Dwight is the third man in the second row.

The officers at West Point stressed discipline. But Ike had a hard time taking some of the many rules seriously. In terms of discipline, he graduated in the bottom fourth of his class. Once an officer discovered that Ike and a friend named Atkins had broken some minor rule. For punishment, the officer told Ike and his friend to report to him that evening in "full-dress coats." Ike knew that meant the complete, formal uniform.

Cadets Eisenhower and Atkins decided to follow the officer's exact words. The two young men put on their dress coats, which had long tails in the back but were cut short across the waist in front. Since the officer had not mentioned any other clothing, they decided to wear nothing else at all! Wearing only their full-dress coats, they marched to the officer's room, saluted, and said, "Sir, Cadets Eisenhower and Atkins report as ordered."

At West Point, as in high school, Eisenhower demonstrated unusual abilities in math. During a class on integral calculus, a difficult branch of mathematics, the instructor decided to have one of the students solve a problem on the blackboard. Because the problem was so tough, he talked for a long time about the proper way to solve it, going so far as giving the correct answer. Figuring that the odds were against his being chosen, Ike didn't bother to listen to the tedious explanation. As luck would have it, the teacher chose him to solve the problem.

Although he couldn't remember any of the things the instructor had said, Ike tried desperately to think of a way to solve the difficult problem. After he had been standing at the board for more than half an hour, a solution finally occurred to him. Writing as quickly as he could, he finally came up with an answer. Immediately, the instructor turned to him angrily.

"Mr. Eisenhower," the teacher said, "it is obvious that you know nothing whatsoever about this problem. You memorized the answer, put down a lot of figures and steps that have no meaning whatsoever, and then wrote out the answer in the hope of fooling the instructor."

Thinking that he was, once again, in serious trouble, Ike was relieved when another teacher, inspecting the class, asked him to go over the solution. After thinking a bit, the other teacher said, "Mr. Eisenhower's solution is more logical and easier than the one we've been using. I'm surprised that none of us, supposedly good mathematicians, has stumbled on it." He went on to say that Ike's solution would be used in classes from that point on.

Opposite page: Eisenhower's 1915
West Point yearbook picture

Left: Ike and Mamie on the steps of Saint Louis College in San Antonio, Texas, in 1916. Opposite page: The Eisenhowers' wedding portrait. Ike would not sit down before the ceremony because he was afraid of creasing his dress slacks.

Ike graduated from the military academy in 1915. After borrowing the money he needed to buy the proper army uniforms, he began working in September of that year as a second lieutenant at Fort Sam Houston, near San Antonio, Texas. On a salary of $141.67 a month, it would take him a while to pay off his debts.

In Texas, he met a pretty young woman named Mamie Doud. Ike and Mamie soon fell in love, and as a sign of their engagement to become married, Ike gave her his class ring on Valentine's Day in 1916. They were married in the Denver home of Mamie's parents the same year. In order to travel to Denver, Ike had to work hard to convince an army officer at Fort Sam Houston to give him a ten-day pass.

Eisenhower (background, right) at Fort Sam Houston with Mexican general Alvaro Obregon (left), bandit Pancho Villa (center), and U.S. general John Pershing (right)

Although Ike's football career at West Point had been shortened by a knee injury, he was known as an expert player. In Houston, a number of small schools asked him to coach their teams in his spare time, and he agreed. But there would soon be little time for games. A number of serious problems were growing, for the United States and the world.

In 1915 and 1916, the Mexican outlaw Pancho Villa had led a gang of outlaws who terrorized towns along the U.S.-Mexican border. The army was called in to restore order. Although Ike applied to join the forces chasing Pancho Villa's gang, the orders were not approved.

By 1917, just a few months after Ike's marriage to Mamie, a far more serious problem was developing. Germany, already at war with a number of European nations, announced that it would renew its submarine warfare against ships from most of the nations of the world. Soon many ships, some from the United States, were sunk by

President Wilson delivers his message declaring war on Germany in 1917.

German torpedoes. In April of 1917, President Woodrow Wilson asked the U.S. Congress to declare war on Germany. World War I had begun.

Throughout the war, Eisenhower expected to receive orders to travel to Europe to fight in the battles that were raging there. But he found instead that he had to serve on military bases at home. For American soldiers at home as well as overseas, the times were rapidly changing.

As they had for generations, many American fighting men still traveled by horseback, by mule, and on foot. But on the battlefields of Europe, on army bases in the U.S., and on the streets of American towns and cities, cars and trucks were appearing in increasing numbers. The airplane, now less than fifteen years old, was already being pressed into service in the war effort. For a time, Ike considered entering the new field of aviation, but because Mamie's family considered airplanes a foolhardy experiment, he eventually decided against it.

At Camp Colt: Eisenhower with officers Clopton, Summers, and Hamond

Instead, Eisenhower was ordered to train American soldiers in the use of one of the newest weapons of war, the armored tank. In March of 1918, at the age of twenty-seven, he was placed in charge of Camp Colt, near Gettysburg, Pennsylvania. At Camp Colt, it was his responsibility to train soldiers to use the new tanks. This proved to be no easy task, since for a long period there were no tanks available for the soldiers at Camp Colt. Nevertheless, Eisenhower managed to train his troops so well that he was eventually given a distinguished service medal.

By November of 1918, just days before Ike was to join the battles overseas, World War I was over. The army suddenly faced the task of releasing millions of soldiers from active duty. Eisenhower, who had reached the rank of lieutenant colonel during the war, was reduced to a captain in the smaller peacetime army. Soon he was promoted to major, a classification he held for sixteen years.

Eisenhower's 1919 truck convoy heading through a pass

In July of 1919, he took part in an army experiment—
driving a convoy of trucks in a coast-to-coast trip across
the United States. At the time, there were no highways and
no real road that stretched all the way across America. As
Eisenhower himself pointed out, the building of the
railroads in the latter half of the nineteenth century had
discouraged overland travel on roads.

The convoy started out on July 7 from a position near
the White House in Washington, D.C. Almost everywhere,
progress was slowed by poor roads and mechanical break-
downs. Although it traveled as fast as possible, the convoy
did not reach San Francisco until September 6, two months
after it had begun. The experience undoubtedly helped
Eisenhower to decide, years later as president, to begin
building a system of superhighways across the U.S. Today,
driving only during daylight, one can travel from Washington, D.C., to San Francisco in less than a week.

General Fox Conner (holding papers) presents Eisenhower (standing alone) with the Distinguished Service Medal in Panama in 1922.

Between 1922 and 1924, Ike served in the army forces stationed at the Panama Canal. There he formed a friendship with General Fox Conner, who was certain that the peace agreements that had ended the First World War were bound to lead to a second. General Conner was so sure of his prediction that he encouraged Ike to continue his studies of military history. Throughout his duties at various military bases in the U.S. and France, Ike never forgot Conner's warning. During this period, he also attended a special army college in Fort Leavenworth, Kansas, where he graduated first in his class of 275 students. Later, he attended the Army War College in Washington.

For an exciting period of a little over a year, Ike had the opportunity to work at a military base in Paris, France, where he learned much about that European country. But

General Douglas MacArthur with his aide, Major Eisenhower

in 1929, the same year that the New York Stock Exchange collapsed and the Great Depression began, he returned to Washington, D.C. There, during the worst years of the Great Depression, he had an important job working with leaders of industry to find out how U.S. factories could be made ready to produce materials and weapons if another war should develop.

In January of 1933, Eisenhower became an aide to one of the most important men in the army, General Douglas MacArthur. For the next six years the two men worked closely together, first in Washington, D.C., and then in the Philippine Islands in the Pacific Ocean. At the time, the Philippines were a U.S. territory, although the U.S. government was planning to grant Philippine independence in the near future.

MacArthur (foreground) and Eisenhower (behind him) in the Philippines

In September of 1935, Eisenhower set sail aboard the steamship *President Harding* for the Philippine Islands. Mamie stayed in Washington so that their son John could complete the eighth grade before traveling on to join him. In the Philippines, Ike worked with General MacArthur instructing local soldiers.

Ike stayed in the Pacific Islands until 1939, and his visit was a relatively happy one. Mamie and John soon came to live with him, and he did what he could to train the local soldiers. For the first time in sixteen years, he was promoted, this time back to the rank of lieutenant colonel. He also took flying lessons and finally learned how to pilot small airplanes. But the good times were overcome by a dark cloud that was passing over Europe. Near the end of his stay, he had what should have been a wonderful job offer. Instead, it was frightening.

The Nazi flag is hoisted over the Westerplatte, a Polish fort and munitions dump, in September 1939 after Hitler's victory there.

Through a number of friends, Ike learned that a group of people were willing to pay him the huge salary of $60,000 a year for this job. If he accepted, he would have to search the world to find new homes for perhaps millions of German Jewish refugees. By 1939, the Nazi government of Adolf Hitler was already at war with the Jewish citizens of Germany, with much of Europe, and soon with most of the world. Just as General Fox Conner had predicted fifteen years earlier, World War II was at hand.

Eisenhower was too devoted to the army to accept the job offer. He knew now that a terrible struggle lay ahead. During the global war, he would rise from an obscure army officer to the most powerful soldier the western world has yet known.

Chapter 4

Hero of the Western World

When German soldiers attacked Poland in September of 1939, World War II began. Certain that the U.S. soon would be involved in the war, Lieutenant Colonel Dwight Eisenhower, his wife Mamie, and their son John set sail from Manila for the United States. They celebrated Christmas in Hawaii and arrived in San Francisco by New Year's Eve. By the early days of 1940, Ike was already at work helping the army organize training camps for soldiers.

Throughout 1940, he showed his skill at organizing the movement of large numbers of troops, as well as feeding, housing, and training them. Throughout 1940 and the early months of 1941, a period during which the U.S. Army was expanding rapidly in preparation for World War II, Ike was given more and more responsibility. By the end of June 1941, he was transferred to Texas, where he soon became chief of staff of the Third Army, an important leadership position in a force of nearly a quarter of a million soldiers.

Opposite page: Ike's homecoming parade
in Washington after Germany surrendered

49

It was in Texas that Eisenhower first became known to the general public. At an important training session where mock battles were fought, a number of newspaper reporters began writing stories telling how carefully and quickly Eisenhower organized his troops. Soon afterward, he was promoted to the position of brigadier general. Although World War II was raging in Europe and Asia, the United States was still officially at peace. The buildup of the army and other branches of the U.S. Armed Forces was simply a precaution in case the U.S. should be drawn into the fighting. Many Americans hoped that it would not be. On December 7, 1941, their hopes were destroyed.

On that day, Ike ate lunch in his office in Texas and then decided to take a nap. He left orders with his assistants that he was not to be awakened for any reason. But his helpers were unable to follow those orders. Shortly, they awoke him with the news that Japanese bombers had attacked Pearl Harbor, an important U.S. naval base in the Hawaiian Islands. Like many of the other countries of the world, the United States was forced to join World War II.

Five days later, a soldier in Washington, D.C., called Ike's Texas office. "The chief says for you to hop a plane and get up here right away," the soldier told him. Ike and Mamie had hoped to travel to West Point, where their son John was a cadet, to celebrate Christmas, but now all that was changed. Mamie quickly packed a suitcase for her husband, who then hurried to the airport.

Ike's plane got only as far as Dallas before it was forced to make an emergency landing. The rest of the long journey to Washington had to be made by train. Brigadier

Ike with General George Marshall (right)

General Eisenhower arrived in Washington on December
14. Immediately, he began working with General George
Marshall, the "chief" referred to in the telephone call, to
make the army's plans for World War II. Working at a
desk job in Washington, Eisenhower was far away from
the battle lines. But that, too, was about to change.

Ike was convinced that the United States would enter
the war in Europe first and then concentrate on the
Japanese in the Pacific later. He drew up plans detailing an
Allied attack on German-controlled Europe, starting from
a point across the English Channel in Britain. General
Marshall seemed impressed by the plan. He asked Ike to
draw up a set of orders for the man to be put in charge of
American forces in Europe, and then he asked for Ike's
recommendation on who that man should be.

Eisenhower points to a map on the office wall of his London headquarters.

Eisenhower suggested a name to General Marshall, but the general seemed to ignore it. Instead, he sent Eisenhower to England, one of the few Western European nations not conquered by the Nazis. In May of 1942, Ike attended a conference in London of the Allied nations planning upcoming battles against the Germans. The following month, he was back in Washington. He placed his final version of the instructions for America's military leader in Europe on Marshall's desk on June 15, 1942.

"Are you satisfied with it?" Marshall reportedly asked Ike. Eisenhower said that he was. Marshall responded that it was a good thing, "because these are the orders you're to operate under. You're in command." Eisenhower had been told to follow his own orders! Ten days later, the commander who had never fought in an actual battle moved into his new headquarters in London.

Field Marshal Erwin Rommel touring the African front in 1941. Nicknamed the "Desert Fox" for his clever tactics, Rommel was accused of plotting to kill Hitler in July 1944. Given the choice of trial or poison, he chose the poison.

"War, as so many men have said, is the most stupid and tragic of human ventures," Ike wrote in one of his books. "It is stupid because so few problems are enduringly solved; tragic because its cost in lives and spirit and treasure is seldom matched in the fruits of victory." By the Fourth of July, 1942, it was obvious that the costs of World War II were going to be staggering.

Almost everywhere they went, German soldiers were enjoying victory after victory. In the west, most of Europe already had been conquered. In the east, the Nazis were fighting fierce battles with the Russians. Two days before the Fourth of July, a huge Russian fortress fell, giving vast new areas of Russian terrritory to the Germans. In the south, the soldiers and tanks of German general Erwin Rommel were racing across North Africa, conquering everyone in their path.

Above: German soldiers rushing into Poland, September 1939
Below: Allied troops march through the African desert in a sand storm

Left to right: Field Marshal Sir Allen Brooke, Chief of Imperial General Staff; General Dwight Eisenhower; British Prime Minister Winston Churchill; and Air Chief Marshal Sir Arthur Tedder

Australian fighters storm
a German stronghold in
the North African desert.

The leaders of the Allied nations, especially Roosevelt
and Churchill, felt they should begin the attacks not in
Europe, but in Africa. During the darkest days of World
War II, Ike planned the massive assault on German forces
in North Africa from his headquarters in England.

"More and more," he wrote, "I came to realize that
brainpower is always in far shorter supply than man-
power." As the first of thousands of tons of equipment
arrived in England from the U.S. in preparation for the
African attack, Ike learned that none of the shipping crates
had been properly labeled. Every box and crate had to be
opened, its contents studied, and then repacked and cor-
rectly labeled. As Allied ships were steaming toward
African Algiers, Ike learned that a ship carrying much of
the communication equipment for the entire force had
been sunk. He quickly ordered essential equipment to be
divided among a number of ships.

President Franklin D. Roosevelt (left) and Eisenhower (behind him) in Sicily

The Allied troops landed on the beaches of North Africa on November 8, 1942. During the invasion, Ike made his headquarters in tunnels under the famous Rock of Gibraltar at the western end of the Mediterranean. Soon he was able to move to Algiers, on the African mainland. In the months that followed, he traveled frequently in a DC-3 plane or in a car several hundred miles eastward to watch the battles that were raging in the deserts of North Africa.

By May of 1943, a considerable portion of North Africa had been captured from Rommel's Nazi troops. Ike soon ordered his troops back into ships, which sailed into the Mediterranean toward the island of Sicily and the Italian peninsula. Sicily was quickly conquered. On September 3, Ike's forces invaded Italy, a nation that had been fighting on the side of Nazi Germany. The Italian government surrendered almost immediately.

Generals Eisenhower, George Patton, Omar Bradley, and Courtney Hodges
in March 1945, "somewhere" in Germany

Eisenhower's smashing victories in Africa and in and around the Mediterranean provided welcome news. Right after one of the battles, he was promoted to the rank of four-star general, the second highest rank attainable in the U.S. Army. A year or so later, he was promoted to the highest rank of all, five-star general. But he had little time to think about his titles. When he attended a Thanksgiving Day planning session in Egypt with General Marshall, he completely forgot that it was a holiday. "I'll be darned," he said over dinner. "Is it Thanksgiving?"

Two days later, Eisenhower received a tattered piece of paper wrapped in plastic from George Marshall. On it were printed the words of a message sent from President Roosevelt to Joseph Stalin, premier of Russia:

> From the President to Marshall Stalin
> The immediate appointment of Eisenhower to command
> Overlord operation has been decided upon   Roosevelt

Because of the success of Operation Overlord in Western Europe, as well as the advances of the Russian army in Eastern Europe, Germany was forced to surrender on May 7, 1945.

On June 12, he returned to London where he was given a triumphant welcome. Less than a week later, he returned to Washington, D.C., where huge crowds strained to catch a glimpse of the famous soldier. After addressing a joint session of Congress in Washington, he traveled to New York City, where four million people cheered at a parade in his honor. Smaller but no less enthusiastic crowds greeted him at his homecoming in Abilene, Kansas, on June 22.

The same year, he was promoted to chief of staff, the highest position in the U.S. Army, with an office in the Pentagon, the headquarters of the U.S. military. On his first day on the job, he got lost in the maze of hallways in the enormous Pentagon building. Many newspapers across the country reported in large headlines that the army's new chief of staff was unable to find his own office.

Despite the humor, there were some serious worries faced by the U.S. military after World War II. In the closing days of the war, the Russian army had marched through Eastern Europe, setting up governments in countries such as Poland, Czechoslovakia, and Hungary that were sure to follow orders from the Russian capital in Moscow.

The Nazis were gone, but many soldiers, including Ike, wondered if a new enemy had not arisen in the once free nations of Eastern Europe.

Eisenhower's installation as president of Columbia University

By 1947, the fifty-seven-year-old general began thinking about retiring from the military. But many other people had plans for the hero of the recent war. A number of people wanted him to run for president of the United States. But rumors that he would become a candidate were put to rest when he accepted an invitation to become the president of Columbia University in New York City instead. He officially became president of the large college on October 12, 1948. At around the same time, he wrote and published his first book, *Crusade in Europe*. His description of the European battles of World War II became an enormous best-seller.

Ike inspects French NATO troops in Koblenz, Germany.

In 1951, he took a leave of absence from Columbia at the request of President Truman so that he could once again travel to Europe. In the limelight yet again, he helped to organize the military command of an important new treaty organization of countries in North America and Europe: the North Atlantic Treaty Organization (NATO). By now, more and more people were calling for him to run for president, even though it was hardly clear whether he was a Republican or a Democrat. Ike stated that he had "a Republican voting record" and might accept a "clear-cut call for political duty," but hardly seemed anxious to become president. But many members of the Republican party had quite different feelings.

Above: Eisenhower poses with his brothers and his parents. Left: Dwight and Mamie Eisenhower with their first child, Doud Dwight Eisenhower, around 1920. The child died of scarlet fever at the age of three.

Right: Mamie pins a medal on Ike in the Philippines. Philippine President Manuel Quezon looks on. Below: The Eisenhowers and their son John leave New York for Washington, D.C., in January 1953, where they will prepare for Ike's inauguration as president.

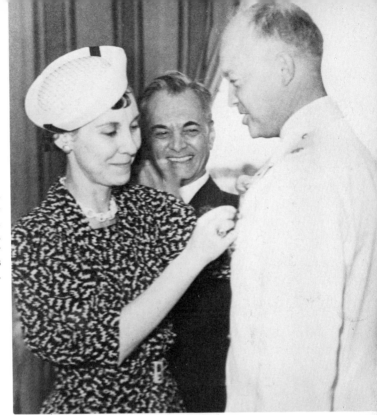

Chapter 5

Thirty-Fourth President

"I like Ike" was a slogan familiar to the nearly thirty-four million Americans who voted for Republican candidate Dwight Eisenhower in the presidential elections of November 4, 1952. For the army general and his vice-presidential running mate, Richard M. Nixon, a U.S. senator from California, it was an easy victory. Adlai Stevenson, the Democratic candidate for president, received only a little more than twenty-seven million votes. For the first time in two decades, Americans had elected a Republican instead of a Democrat for president.

By the time they reach the highest office in the land, most American presidents have held a variety of political offices. But the presidency was Eisenhower's first job in politics. Many people thought that Ike would be a moderate, "middle of the road" politician, but he surprised them. He soon showed that he was strongly conservative.

President Eisenhower poses with his new cabinet members.

Ike's conservatism was shown by the men he chose to join his cabinet, his group of top advisers. He picked rich, successful businesspeople for his cabinet. For his secretary of defense, he named Charles E. Wilson, the president of the huge firm of General Motors. Other wealthy businesspeople, including the wife of a Texas publisher, were selected for other cabinet posts. Only for secretary of labor did he select a man who wasn't a millionaire. The new labor secretary, Martin Durkin, had been president of the International Plumbers Union. One writer quipped that the president's cabinet was made up of "eight millionaires and a plumber." The following year, the plumber resigned. The people Eisenhower chose for his cabinet helped America enter perhaps the most prosperous era in its history. But there was an immediate problem facing the new president when he took office.

Rubble litters the streets of Seoul as UN forces recapture the city.

Since the end of World War II, the Asian peninsula of Korea had been divided into two nations. North Korea was controlled by a Communist government, but South Korea was not. On June 25, 1950, when Ike was still the president of Columbia University, war broke out in Korea. At 4:00 that morning, Communist soldiers crossed their southern border and attacked South Korea. To many people throughout the world, the attack proved that the Communists, led by the Soviet Union and China, would use force to make as much of the world Communist as possible.

Armies from the United Nations, principally the United States, entered Korea and attempted to stop the invasion from the north. But by 1951, more than half a million Communist Chinese soldiers had also entered the war, fighting against the UN forces. By the middle of 1951, peace talks were under way, but the fighting dragged on as neither side seemed able to win a clear victory.

Ike in South Korea in December 1952

Most Americans still remembered the sacrifices they had made during World War II. They were in no mood for yet another long war. While campaigning for the presidency in 1951, Ike promised "an early and honorable end" to the Korean War. "I shall go to Korea," he promised, in order to end the conflict.

After the election, he lost little time keeping his promise. On November 29, 1952, nearly two months before he officially became president, he made a secret trip to Korea to inspect the fighting. Many military men, especially General Douglas MacArthur, seemed to favor enlarging the war. Ike traveled to the front lines and, using the experience he had gained from his years in the army, determined that a complete victory could not be gained at the time. He decided to wait, not widening the war but making sure that the Communists were kept from advancing into South Korea again.

President Eisenhower delivering his inaugural address

During his first inaugural address in Washington, the new president said: "Americans, indeed all free men, remember that in the final choice a soldier's pack is not so heavy a burden as a prisoner's chains." But for the time being, it appeared as if the burdensome war in Korea would last for some time.

Fortunately, the new president did not have to wait long to honor his promise of peace. A little more than three months after Ike took office, Joseph Stalin, the premier of Russia, died. A few weeks later, the Communist leaders of North Korea expressed an interest in ending the war. A truce was signed in July. The war was over, but the new American president and millions of other people now felt certain that Communist governments offered a serious threat to the peace and security of the world. During his announcement that the fighting was over, Ike warned: "We must not relax our guard."

The fear of Communism in the U.S. Congress reached fanatic heights during the first year of Eisenhower's administration. Since 1950, a U.S. senator named Joseph McCarthy had been making a name for himself by exposing people he suspected of being Communist sympathizers. Before long, he had developed lengthy files on writers, actors, politicians, government workers, and many others who seemed to have even a remote tie to a Communist or Socialist cause. As a result, many people were unable to find jobs simply because McCarthy had branded them as "Communists" or "Communist sympathizers." Some were even blacklisted, or kept from working, for refusing to answer pointed and often unfair questions.

In a nation proud of its freedoms, "McCarthyism," as the senator's movement is called, was most peculiar. For a time, it appeared as if Americans were free to express their own opinions as long as those opinions agreed with the beliefs of Senator McCarthy. McCarthyism placed President Eisenhower in a difficult position.

Like Senator McCarthy, Ike also worried about the growing power of Communist governments in many areas of the world. For a time during 1952, Senator McCarthy traveled on Eisenhower's campaign train. Richard Nixon, Ike's vice-president, was elected to the U.S. Senate in 1950 by following the anti-Communist principles of McCarthyism.

There were, however, great differences between Joseph McCarthy and Dwight Eisenhower. McCarthy, a career politician, used his anti-Communist crusade to attain personal power. Eisenhower, a career soldier who had entered

Joe McCarthy displays a copy of the *Daily Worker*, the Communist party newspaper.

politics reluctantly, desired less power, not more. Ike was known for dealing with people fairly and without anger. Joe McCarthy was just the opposite.

President Eisenhower knew throughout his first year in office that McCarthy's attacks against innocent Americans were unjust. But Ike's conservative principles included a belief in limited powers of the presidency. He refused to get into congressional politics, at least until 1954.

That year, McCarthy began searching for Communists in the U.S. Army. Before long, he had found an ex-army dentist who had refused to sign a loyalty oath. McCarthy felt that the dentist offered such a threat to America's security that he called in a brigadier general to testify. When the general refused to answer certain questions, McCarthy shouted at him, "You are a disgrace to the uniform. You're shielding Communist(s). . . . You're not fit to be an officer. You're ignorant."

Suddenly, Eisenhower had seen and heard enough. The senator was attacking Ike's own branch of the military, the U.S. Army. It was the army, under Ike's command, that had fought its way through Europe to win World War II from Hitler. The attacks were too much.

In a carefully planned move, Ike's administration let Joseph McCarthy destroy his own career. They did it by using the relatively new but already powerful communications device called television. On the broadcasts of the army-McCarthy hearings from Washington, skilled army lawyers brought out the worst of McCarthy's unfair attacks. Startled Americans, watching television in their living rooms for the first time, saw how the senator bullied witnesses and tried to present half-truths as proof of reckless charges. Soon the entire Senate voted to condemn McCarthy. For the most part, McCarthyism became a peculiar and distasteful episode in American history.

Several other events occurred in 1954 that were of critical importance to the nation. With Eisenhower's urging, Congress passed a tax reform bill nearly a thousand pages long, and he signed it into law. The new tax laws greatly stimulated business, and the American economy went into a long period of rapid growth. Within two years, and for the first time ever, there were more Americans in middle-class jobs such as business management and the professions than there were in factories and other areas of labor. With more money to spend, Americans by the millions began leaving their apartments in the cities and moving to new homes in the suburbs. By the mid-1950s, suburbs were growing seven times as fast as the inner cities.

Waiting for seats at Supreme Court segregation hearings in December 1953

Also in 1954, one of the most important Supreme Court rulings in American history was handed down. That year, in a case called *Brown vs. Board of Education of Topeka*, the Supreme Court decided that American public schools had to be integrated. Since 1898, the court had held that black students could be sent to schools separate from the schools white students attended, as long as they were equally as good as the schools for whites. For fifty-six years, "separate but equal" schools for white and black students were permitted under the law of the land. But in 1954, the court stated that, by their very nature, separate schools were unequal schools.

At first, the Supreme Court decision seemed to have little effect on the Eisenhower administration. But during Ike's second term, the ruling gave him one of his most severe tests of leadership.

During the summer months of 1955, nationwide polls indicated that Ike was one of the most popular presidents in American history. A poll taken that summer showed that even 60 percent of Democratic voters wanted Ike to be the candidate of their party! During the same summer, Ike became the first U.S. president to be shown on the newly developed system called color television. His speech at a class reunion at West Point was shown in color by NBC television on June 7.

While he was vacationing in Denver, Colorado, on September 24, 1955, President Eisenhower suffered a serious heart attack. For more than a month, he remained in bed at Fitzsimons Army Hospital in Denver. A group of administration leaders in Washington headed by Vice-President Nixon, along with other members of the administration, gathered in Denver and did the best they could to carry on Ike's work.

For weeks, television and radio broadcasts as well as newspaper stories from around the country reported every detail of the presidential heartbeat, pulse, and breathing. Many Americans wondered if Ike would be healthy enough to run for a second term. He had been troubled by health problems before. A number of times during his career, he had suffered from painful bouts with ileitis, a disease of the intestine. Later, while still in the White House, he would suffer a slight stroke.

Eisenhower in Denver
in December 1955,
recuperating from
his heart attack

Tens of thousands of letters and telegrams arrived at the army hospital in Denver wishing the president a speedy recovery. "It really does something for you," Ike told Mamie, "to know that people all over the world are praying for you." For months, even Eisenhower himself was not certain that he was healthy enough to run for a second term. But after nearly seven weeks, he was well enough to leave the hospital and fly back to Washington.

By early in 1956, his doctors reported that his heart had healed, and on February 29, 1956, he announced that he would be "available" for a second term. Despite the fact that he needed an operation for ileitis just a few months later, the public seemed satisfied that Ike was healthy.

Soviet tanks in the streets of Budapest, Hungary, during the Hungarian revolt

To the surprise of no one, the president and vice-president easily won the nominations at the Republican convention in 1956. Adlai Stevenson again won the Democratic nomination, with Massachusetts senator John F. Kennedy narrowly missing the vice-presidential nomination.

In the closing days of the 1956 campaign season, disheartening news arrived from a number of far-flung places. Early in November, the world was shocked by television pictures of Russian tanks and troops marching into the small nation of Hungary. A few days earlier, a number of Hungarians had revolted against their own Soviet-dominated government. Now a huge army of Russian soldiers cruelly crushed the rebellion.

A peaceful scene on the Suez Canal in the early 1960s

At almost the same time, a dispute in the Middle East caused the president of Egypt to close the important Suez Canal. On October 31, troops from England and France drove the Egyptian soldiers away from the waterway. Israeli troops were already fighting Egyptians. Soon, the Soviet Union was threatening to intervene. Under Eisenhower's leadership, the U.S. government condemned the "gunboat diplomacy" of the British and French and demanded that Israeli troops leave Egyptian territory. On election day in the United States, the British and French troops agreed to a cease-fire and the Israeli troops left Egypt. None of the countries involved were particularly happy, but a serious threat to world peace had been overcome. Many Republicans pointed out that Ike was the man to trust in a time of crisis.

Arkansas governor
Orval Faubus speaks
to reporters about
the Little Rock
Central High School
integration order.

As he had in 1952, Eisenhower easily defeated Stevenson in the 1956 presidential elections. Still, despite the landslide election for the president, both houses of Congress remained in Democratic control.

Ike once wrote, "There must be no second class citizens in this country." During the first year of his new term in office, he was faced with a supreme test of that ideal. Three years earlier, in 1954, the Supreme Court had ruled that American public schools had to be integrated.

Early in September 1957, nine black students were planning to enter Central High School in Little Rock, Arkansas. With little warning, Arkansas governor Orval Faubus suddenly decided to stop them. Claiming that he was only trying to avoid violence, the governor called on members of the Arkansas National Guard to stand in front of the building and prevent the black students from entering it. Following the advice of the school's superintendent, none of the black students came to school.

The Arkansas National Guard, under Faubus's orders, patrols the entrance to Central High.

At a hastily called meeting between Faubus and President Eisenhower, the president demanded enforcement of the Supreme Court decision. During the meeting at Ike's vacation headquarters in Rhode Island, Faubus seemed to back down. But when he returned to Arkansas, the governor once again called for the National Guard to keep the black students out of the all-white school.

A federal court order demanded the removal of the troops from the school grounds. But now the city's atmosphere was so charged with emotion that the threat of mass violence was severe. Using the powers of the presidency, Eisenhower put the National Guard under his command and sent an army unit of the 101st Airborne Division to Little Rock to preserve the peace and enforce the new desegregation law. On the morning of September 25, 1957, in front of hundreds of reporters, cameramen, soldiers, politicians, and onlookers, nine black students bravely walked into Little Rock Central High School.

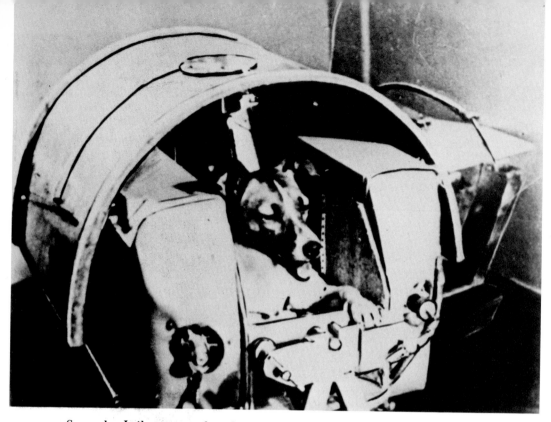

Space dog Laika contemplates her upcoming trip in her *Sputnik* cabin.

Just a month earlier, Ike had signed the first civil rights law passed by Congress in eighty-two years. The law gave the federal government more power to protect people's right to vote. He signed another civil rights bill in 1960. Even earlier, in December 1955, a young minister named Dr. Martin Luther King, Jr., attracted national attention in a demonstration in Montgomery, Alabama. The civil rights movement had begun.

On October 4, 1957, just ten days after the black students first entered Little Rock High School, Russian scientists shocked the world by launching *Sputnik*, the world's first artificial satellite. A month later, they launched *Sputnik II*, which carried a live dog into space. Americans, proud of their scientific achievements, were alarmed to learn that they had fallen behind in the space race.

Explorer I takes off.

In response to the Soviet challenge, Ike appointed a special assistant for science and technology. For some time, the U.S. Navy had been trying to develop a satellite program. Growing impatient with the navy's many failures, Ike called for the army to develop a program of its own. In just three months, an army rocket launched America's first successful artificial satellite, *Explorer.*

A number of other exciting events occurred during Eisenhower's second term. As a result of a law he had worked hard for and had signed in 1956, the construction of America's interstate highway system was vastly acceler-ated. Ike proudly described the massive effort as "the big-gest peacetime construction project of any description ever undertaken by the United States or any other country."

The new $12,000,000 Buffalo (New York) Skyway

When the project began, only New York, Los Angeles, and Chicago had high-speed expressways. The Pennsylvania Turnpike and a few other eastern toll roads were the only four-lane highways between major American cities. When the system was completed around 1980, fast, modern expressways connected most major cities.

On September 26, 1957, Ike became the first American president to travel under the surface of the ocean in a nuclear-powered submarine, the *Seawolf*. A little more than a year later, on January 3, 1959, Alaska became the forty-ninth state. Less than two months later, Ike signed the legislation making Hawaii the fiftieth state in the Union.

During the final years of his administration, the country was troubled by a business recession. Ike remained one of

Ike peers through the *Seawolf*'s periscope.

the most personally popular presidents in American history, but some Americans began to feel that it was time for a change. By law, American presidents could remain in office for only two terms, and Ike certainly was not interested in a third.

During his final months in office, Ike visited many foreign countries. In his final speech as president, he urged Americans to maintain a strong military but to avoid unwise expenses. "An immense military establishment and a large arms industry is new in the American experience," he warned. "We must never let the weight of this combination endanger our liberties or democratic processes. We should take nothing for granted."

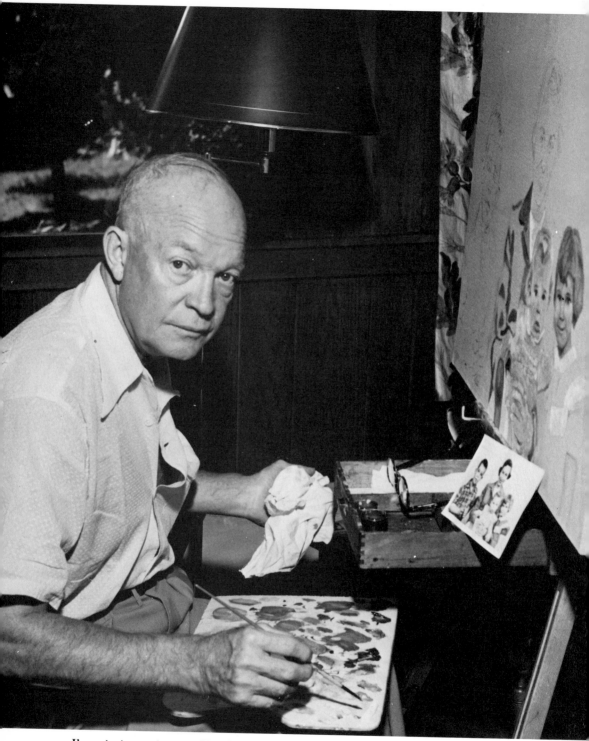

Ike painting a picture of his daughter-in-law, Barbara, and her three children at Camp David, Maryland, August 1954

The Eisenhower residence on their Gettysburg, Pennsylvania, farm. In the foreground
is the golf green that was installed shortly before this 1955 photograph was taken.

Chapter 6

Gettysburg

On January 20, 1961, Dwight D. Eisenhower left office at the age of seventy. At the time, he was the oldest president in America's history. On the same day, John F. Kennedy, the youngest president in American history, took the oath of office to become the thirty-fifth president of the United States. Ike and Mamie moved to a farm they had owned for years near Gettysburg, Pennsylvania, the site of a famous battle during the Civil War.

After fifty years of service to his country, it took a while for Ike to become used to retirement. When he left the White House, he did not know how to use a dial telephone and he didn't have a driver's license. For about two years, his son John lived on the Gettysburg farm to help Ike and Mamie in the transition to private life.

For about three years, the former president worked on a series of books about his experiences in public service. *The White House Years* and *Waging Peace* were written with the help of a team of researchers. Ike worked alone on another book, *At Ease: Stories I Tell to Friends,* and many readers thought it was his very best.

Ike's grandson, David Eisenhower, fishing for flying trout on the Gettysburg farm

Although he had officially retired from politics, politicians constantly sought his help and support. One of them was Richard Nixon, his former vice-president, who eventually become the thirty-seventh president. Although Ike publicly praised Nixon, he always kept his enthusiasm well under control. It is easy to understand why political candidates sought his praise. Throughout 1967 and 1968, years after he had left office, opinion polls indicated that Ike was the most admired man in America.

Little more than a year before he died, the former president made one more glittering achievement. Interested in sports throughout his life, Ike was an avid golf player during his later years. On February 6, 1968, he shot a hole-in-one on a golf course in Palm Springs, California.

Changing of the guard at Eisenhower's funeral in the Capitol building

After a series of heart attacks, he passed away on March 28, 1969, and was buried in his old home town of Abilene, Kansas. "America will be a lonely land without him," said President Lyndon Johnson. "But America will always be a better nation—stronger, safer, more conscious of its heritage, more certain of its destiny—because Ike was with us when America needed him."

Chronology of American History

(Shaded area covers events in Dwight D. Eisenhower's lifetime.)

About A.D. 982 — Eric the Red, born in Norway, reaches Greenland in one of the first European voyages to North America.

About 1000 — Leif Ericson (Eric the Red's son) leads what is thought to be the first European expedition to mainland North America; Leif probably lands in Canada.

1492 — Christopher Columbus, seeking a sea route from Spain to the Far East, discovers the New World.

1497 — John Cabot reaches Canada in the first English voyage to North America.

1513 — Ponce de Léon explores Florida in search of the fabled Fountain of Youth.

1519-1521 — Hernando Cortés of Spain conquers Mexico.

1534 — French explorers led by Jacques Cartier enter the Gulf of St. Lawrence in Canada.

1540 — Spanish explorer Francisco Coronado begins exploring the American Southwest, seeking the riches of the mythical Seven Cities of Cibola.

1565 — St. Augustine, Florida, the first permanent European town in what is now the United States, is founded by the Spanish.

1607 — Jamestown, Virginia, is founded, the first permanent English town in the present-day U.S.

1608 — Frenchman Samuel de Champlain founds the village of Quebec, Canada.

1609 — Henry Hudson explores the eastern coast of present-day U.S. for the Netherlands; the Dutch then claim parts of New York, New Jersey, Delaware, and Connecticut and name the area New Netherland.

1619 — The English colonies' first shipment of black slaves arrives in Jamestown.

1620 — English Pilgrims found Massachusetts' first permanent town at Plymouth.

1621 — Massachusetts Pilgrims and Indians hold the famous first Thanksgiving feast in colonial America.

1623 — Colonization of New Hampshire is begun by the English.

1624 — Colonization of present-day New York State is begun by the Dutch at Fort Orange (Albany).

1625 — The Dutch start building New Amsterdam (now New York City).

1630 — The town of Boston, Massachusetts, is founded by the English Puritans.

1633 — Colonization of Connecticut is begun by the English.

1634 — Colonization of Maryland is begun by the English.

1636 — Harvard, the colonies' first college, is founded in Massachusetts. Rhode Island colonization begins when Englishman Roger Williams founds Providence.

1638 — Delaware colonization begins as Swedes build Fort Christina at present-day Wilmington.

1640 — Stephen Daye of Cambridge, Massachusetts prints *The Bay Psalm Book*, the first English-language book published in what is now the U.S.

1643 — Swedish settlers begin colonizing Pennsylvania.

About 1650 — North Carolina is colonized by Virginia settlers.

1660 — New Jersey colonization is begun by the Dutch at present-day Jersey City.

1670 — South Carolina colonization is begun by the English near Charleston.

1673 — Jacques Marquette and Louis Jolliet explore the upper Mississippi River for France.

1682—Philadelphia, Pennsylvania, is settled. La Salle explores Mississippi River all the way to its mouth in Louisiana and claims the whole Mississippi Valley for France.

1693—College of William and Mary is founded in Williamsburg, Virginia.

1700—Colonial population is about 250,000.

1703—Benjamin Franklin is born in Boston.

1732—George Washington, first president of the U.S., is born in Westmoreland County, Virginia.

1733—James Oglethorpe founds Savannah, Georgia; Georgia is established as the thirteenth colony.

1735—John Adams, second president of the U.S., is born in Braintree, Massachusetts.

1737—William Byrd founds Richmond, Virginia.

1738—British troops are sent to Georgia over border dispute with Spain.

1739—Black insurrection takes place in South Carolina.

1740—English Parliament passes act allowing naturalization of immigrants to American colonies after seven-year residence.

1743—Thomas Jefferson is born in Albemarle County, Virginia. Benjamin Franklin retires at age thirty-seven to devote himself to scientific inquiries and public service.

1744—King George's War begins; France joins war effort against England.

1745—During King George's War, France raids settlements in Maine and New York.

1747—Classes begin at Princeton College in New Jersey.

1748—The Treaty of Aix-la-Chapelle concludes King George's War.

1749—Parliament legally recognizes slavery in colonies and the inauguration of the plantation system in the South. George Washington becomes the surveyor for Culpepper County in Virginia.

1750—Thomas Walker passes through and names Cumberland Gap on his way toward Kentucky region. Colonial population is about 1,200,000.

1751—James Madison, fourth president of the U.S., is born in Port Conway, Virginia. English Parliament passes Currency Act, banning New England colonies from issuing paper money. George Washington travels to Barbados.

1752—Pennsylvania Hospital, the first general hospital in the colonies, is founded in Philadelphia. Benjamin Franklin uses a kite in a thunderstorm to demonstrate that lightning is a form of electricity.

1753—George Washington delivers command that the French withdraw from the Ohio River Valley; French disregard the demand. Colonial population is about 1,328,000.

1754—French and Indian War begins (extends to Europe as the Seven Years' War). Washington surrenders at Fort Necessity.

1755—French and Indians ambush Braddock. Washington becomes commander of Virginia troops.

1756—England declares war on France.

1758—James Monroe, fifth president of the U.S., is born in Westmoreland County, Virginia.

1759—Cherokee Indian war begins in southern colonies; hostilities extend to 1761. George Washington marries Martha Dandridge Custis.

1760—George III becomes king of England. Colonial population is about 1,600,000.

1762—England declares war on Spain.

1763—Treaty of Paris concludes the French and Indian War and the Seven Years' War. England gains Canada and most other French lands east of the Mississippi River.

1764—British pass the Sugar Act to gain tax money from the colonists. The issue of taxation without representation is first introduced in Boston. John Adams marries Abigail Smith.

1765—Stamp Act goes into effect in the colonies. Business virtually stops as almost all colonists refuse to use the stamps.

1766—British repeal the Stamp Act.

1767—John Quincy Adams, sixth president of the U.S. and son of second president John Adams, is born in Braintree, Massachusetts. Andrew Jackson, seventh president of the U.S., is born in Waxhaw settlement, South Carolina.

1769—Daniel Boone sights the Kentucky Territory.

1770—In the Boston Massacre, British soldiers kill five colonists and injure six. Townshend Acts are repealed, thus eliminating all duties on imports to the colonies except tea.

1771—Benjamin Franklin begins his autobiography, a work that he will never complete. The North Carolina assembly passes the "Bloody Act," which makes rioters guilty of treason.

1772—Samuel Adams rouses colonists to consider British threats to self-government.

1773—English Parliament passes the Tea Act. Colonists dressed as Mohawk Indians board British tea ships and toss 342 casks of tea into the water in what becomes known as the Boston Tea Party. William Henry Harrison is born in Charles City County, Virginia.

1774—British close the port of Boston to punish the city for the Boston Tea Party. First Continental Congress convenes in Philadelphia.

1775—American Revolution begins with battles of Lexington and Concord, Massachusetts. Second Continental Congress opens in Philadelphia. George Washington becomes commander-in-chief of the Continental army.

1776—Declaration of Independence is adopted on July 4.

1777—Congress adopts the American flag with thirteen stars and thirteen stripes. John Adams is sent to France to negotiate peace treaty.

1778—France declares war against Great Britain and becomes U.S. ally.

1779—British surrender to Americans at Vincennes. Thomas Jefferson is elected governor of Virginia. James Madison is elected to the Continental Congress.

1780—Benedict Arnold, first American traitor, defects to the British.

1781—Articles of Confederation go into effect. Cornwallis surrenders to George Washington at Yorktown, ending the American Revolution.

1782—American commissioners, including John Adams, sign peace treaty with British in Paris. Thomas Jefferson's wife, Martha, dies. Martin Van Buren is born in Kinderhook, New York.

1784—Zachary Taylor is born near Barboursville, Virginia.

1785—Congress adopts the dollar as the unit of currency. John Adams is made minister to Great Britain. Thomas Jefferson is appointed minister to France.

1786—Shays's Rebellion begins in Massachusetts.

1787—Constitutional Convention assembles in Philadelphia, with George Washington presiding; U.S. Constitution is adopted. Delaware, New Jersey, and Pennsylvania become states.

1788—Virginia, South Carolina, New York, Connecticut, New Hampshire, Maryland, and Massachusetts become states. U.S. Constitution is ratified. New York City is declared U.S. capital.

1789—Presidential electors elect George Washington and John Adams as first president and vice-president. Thomas Jefferson is appointed secretary of state. North Carolina becomes a state. French Revolution begins.

1790—Supreme Court meets for the first time. Rhode Island becomes a state. First national census in the U.S. counts 3,929,214 persons. John Tyler is born in Charles City County, Virginia.

1791—Vermont enters the Union. U.S. Bill of Rights, the first ten amendments to the Constitution, goes into effect. District of Columbia is established. James Buchanan is born in Stony Batter, Pennsylvania.

1792—Thomas Paine publishes *The Rights of Man.* Kentucky becomes a state. Two political parties are formed in the U.S., Federalist and Republican. Washington is elected to a second term, with Adams as vice-president.

1793—War between France and Britain begins; U.S. declares neutrality. Eli Whitney invents the cotton gin; cotton production and slave labor increase in the South.

92

1794—Eleventh Amendment to the Constitution is passed, limiting federal courts' power. "Whiskey Rebellion" in Pennsylvania protests federal whiskey tax. James Madison marries Dolley Payne Todd.

1795—George Washington signs the Jay Treaty with Great Britain. Treaty of San Lorenzo, between U.S. and Spain, settles Florida boundary and gives U.S. right to navigate the Mississippi. James Polk is born near Pineville, North Carolina.

1796—Tennessee enters the Union. Washington gives his Farewell Address, refusing a third presidential term. John Adams is elected president and Thomas Jefferson vice-president.

1797—Adams recommends defense measures against possible war with France. Napoleon Bonaparte and his army march against Austrians in Italy. U.S. population is about 4,900,000.

1798—Washington is named commander-in-chief of the U.S. Army. Department of the Navy is created. Alien and Sedition Acts are passed. Napoleon's troops invade Egypt and Switzerland.

1799—George Washington dies at Mount Vernon, New York. James Monroe is elected governor of Virginia. French Revolution ends. Napoleon becomes ruler of France.

1800—Thomas Jefferson and Aaron Burr tie for president. U.S. capital is moved from Philadelphia to Washington, D.C. The White House is built as presidents' home. Spain returns Louisiana to France. Millard Fillmore is born in Locke, New York.

1801—After thirty-six ballots, House of Representatives elects Thomas Jefferson president, making Burr vice-president. James Madison is named secretary of state.

1802—Congress abolishes excise taxes. U.S. Military Academy is founded at West Point, New York.

1803—Ohio enters the Union. Louisiana Purchase treaty is signed with France, greatly expanding U.S. territory.

1804—Twelfth Amendment to the Constitution rules that president and vice-president be elected separately. Alexander Hamilton is killed by Vice-President Aaron Burr in a duel. Orleans Territory is established. Napoleon crowns himself emperor of France. Franklin Pierce is born in Hillsborough Lower Village, New Hampshire.

1805—Thomas Jefferson begins his second term as president. Lewis and Clark expedition reaches the Pacific Ocean.

1806—Coinage of silver dollars is stopped; resumes in 1836.

1807—Aaron Burr is acquitted in treason trial. Embargo Act closes U.S. ports to trade.

1808—James Madison is elected president. Congress outlaws importing slaves from Africa. Andrew Johnson is born in Raleigh, North Carolina.

1809—Abraham Lincoln is born near Hodgenville, Kentucky.

1810—U.S. population is 7,240,000.

1811—William Henry Harrison defeats Indians at Tippecanoe. Monroe is named secretary of state.

1812—Louisiana becomes a state. U.S. declares war on Britain (War of 1812). James Madison is reelected president. Napoleon invades Russia.

1813—British forces take Fort Niagara and Buffalo, New York.

1814—Francis Scott Key writes "The Star-Spangled Banner." British troops burn much of Washington, D.C., including the White House. Treaty of Ghent ends War of 1812. James Monroe becomes secretary of war.

1815—Napoleon meets his final defeat at Battle of Waterloo.

1816—James Monroe is elected president. Indiana becomes a state.

1817—Mississippi becomes a state. Construction on Erie Canal begins.

1818—Illinois enters the Union. The present thirteen-stripe flag is adopted. Border between U.S. and Canada is agreed upon.

1819—Alabama becomes a state. U.S. purchases Florida from Spain. Thomas Jefferson establishes the University of Virginia.

1820—James Monroe is reelected. In the Missouri Compromise, Maine enters the Union as a free (non-slave) state.

1821—Missouri enters the Union as a slave state. Santa Fe Trail opens the American Southwest. Mexico declares independence from Spain. Napoleon Bonaparte dies.

1822—U.S. recognizes Mexico and Colombia. Liberia in Africa is founded as a home for freed slaves. Ulysses S. Grant is born in Point Pleasant, Ohio. Rutherford B. Hayes is born in Delaware, Ohio.

1823—Monroe Doctrine closes North and South America to European colonizing or invasion.

1824—House of Representatives elects John Quincy Adams president when none of the four candidates wins a majority in national election. Mexico becomes a republic.

1825—Erie Canal is opened. U.S. population is 11,300,000.

1826—Thomas Jefferson and John Adams both die on July 4, the fiftieth anniversary of the Declaration of Independence.

1828—Andrew Jackson is elected president. Tariff of Abominations is passed, cutting imports.

1829—James Madison attends Virginia's constitutional convention. Slavery is abolished in Mexico. Chester A. Arthur is born in Fairfield, Vermont.

1830—Indian Removal Act to resettle Indians west of the Mississippi is approved.

1831—James Monroe dies in New York City. James A. Garfield is born in Orange, Ohio. Cyrus McCormick develops his reaper.

1832—Andrew Jackson, nominated by the new Democratic Party, is reelected president.

1833—Britain abolishes slavery in its colonies. Benjamin Harrison is born in North Bend, Ohio.

1835—Federal government becomes debt-free for the first time.

1836—Martin Van Buren becomes president. Texas wins independence from Mexico. Arkansas joins the Union. James Madison dies at Montpelier, Virginia.

1837—Michigan enters the Union. U.S. population is 15,900,000. Grover Cleveland is born in Caldwell, New Jersey.

1840—William Henry Harrison is elected president.

1841—President Harrison dies in Washington, D.C., one month after inauguration. Vice-President John Tyler succeeds him.

1843—William McKinley is born in Niles, Ohio.

1844—James Knox Polk is elected president. Samuel Morse sends first telegraphic message.

1845—Texas and Florida become states. Potato famine in Ireland causes massive emigration from Ireland to U.S. Andrew Jackson dies near Nashville, Tennessee.

1846—Iowa enters the Union. War with Mexico begins.

1847—U.S. captures Mexico City.

1848—John Quincy Adams dies in Washington, D.C. Zachary Taylor becomes president. Treaty of Guadalupe Hidalgo ends Mexico-U.S. war. Wisconsin becomes a state.

1849—James Polk dies in Nashville, Tennessee.

1850—President Taylor dies in Washington, D.C.; Vice-President Millard Fillmore succeeds him. California enters the Union, breaking tie between slave and free states.

1852—Franklin Pierce is elected president.

1853—Gadsden Purchase transfers Mexican territory to U.S.

1854—"War for Bleeding Kansas" is fought between slave and free states.

1855—Czar Nicholas I of Russia dies, succeeded by Alexander II.

1856—James Buchanan is elected president. In Massacre of Potawatomi Creek, Kansas-slavers are murdered by free-staters. Woodrow Wilson is born in Staunton, Virginia.

1857—William Howard Taft is born in Cincinnati, Ohio.

1858—Minnesota enters the Union. Theodore Roosevelt is born in New York City.

1859—Oregon becomes a state.

1860—Abraham Lincoln is elected president; South Carolina secedes from the Union in protest.

1861—Arkansas, Tennessee, North Carolina, and Virginia secede. Kansas enters the Union as a free state. Civil War begins.

1862—Union forces capture Fort Henry, Roanoke Island, Fort Donelson, Jacksonville, and New Orleans; Union armies are defeated at the battles of Bull Run and Fredericksburg. Martin Van Buren dies in Kinderhook, New York. John Tyler dies near Charles City, Virginia.

1863—Lincoln issues Emancipation Proclamation: all slaves held in rebelling territories are declared free. West Virginia becomes a state.

1864—Abraham Lincoln is reelected. Nevada becomes a state.

1865—Lincoln is assassinated in Washington, D.C., and succeeded by Andrew Johnson. U.S. Civil War ends on May 26. Thirteenth Amendment abolishes slavery. Warren G. Harding is born in Blooming Grove, Ohio.

1867—Nebraska becomes a state. U.S. buys Alaska from Russia for $7,200,000. Reconstruction Acts are passed.

1868—President Johnson is impeached for violating Tenure of Office Act, but is acquitted by Senate. Ulysses S. Grant is elected president. Fourteenth Amendment prohibits voting discrimination. James Buchanan dies in Lancaster, Pennsylvania.

1869—Franklin Pierce dies in Concord, New Hampshire.

1870—Fifteenth Amendment gives blacks the right to vote.

1872—Grant is reelected over Horace Greeley. General Amnesty Act pardons ex-Confederates. Calvin Coolidge is born in Plymouth Notch, Vermont.

1874—Millard Fillmore dies in Buffalo, New York. Herbert Hoover is born in West Branch, Iowa.

1875—Andrew Johnson dies in Carter's Station, Tennessee.

1876—Colorado enters the Union. "Custer's last stand": he and his men are massacred by Sioux Indians at Little Big Horn, Montana.

1877—Rutherford B. Hayes is elected president as all disputed votes are awarded to him.

1880—James A. Garfield is elected president.

1881—President Garfield is assassinated and dies in Elberon, New Jersey. Vice-President Chester A. Arthur succeeds him.

1882—U.S. bans Chinese immigration. Franklin D. Roosevelt is born in Hyde Park, New York.

1884—Grover Cleveland is elected president. Harry S. Truman is born in Lamar, Missouri.

1885—Ulysses S. Grant dies in Mount McGregor, New York.

1886—Statue of Liberty is dedicated. Chester A. Arthur dies in New York City.

1888—Benjamin Harrison is elected president.

1889—North Dakota, South Dakota, Washington, and Montana become states.

1890—Dwight D. Eisenhower is born in Denison, Texas. Idaho and Wyoming become states.

1892—Grover Cleveland is elected president.

1893—Rutherford B. Hayes dies in Fremont, Ohio.

1896—William McKinley is elected president. Utah becomes a state.

1898—U.S. declares war on Spain over Cuba.

1900—McKinley is reelected. Boxer Rebellion against foreigners in China begins.

1901—McKinley is assassinated by anarchist Leon Czolgosz in Buffalo, New York; Theodore Roosevelt becomes president. Benjamin Harrison dies in Indianapolis, Indiana.

1902—U.S. acquires perpetual control over Panama Canal.

1903—Alaskan frontier is settled.

1904—Russian-Japanese War breaks out. Theodore Roosevelt wins presidential election.

1905—Treaty of Portsmouth signed, ending Russian-Japanese War.

1906—U.S. troops occupy Cuba.

1907—President Roosevelt bars all Japanese immigration. Oklahoma enters the Union.

1908—William Howard Taft becomes president. Grover Cleveland dies in Princeton, New Jersey. Lyndon B. Johnson is born near Stonewall, Texas.

1909—NAACP is founded under W.E.B. DuBois

1910—China abolishes slavery.

1911—Chinese Revolution begins. Ronald Reagan is born in Tampico, Illinois.

1912—Woodrow Wilson is elected president. Arizona and New Mexico become states.

1913—Federal income tax is introduced in U.S. through the Sixteenth Amendment. Richard Nixon is born in Yorba Linda, California. Gerald Ford is born in Omaha, Nebraska.

1914—World War I begins.

1915—British liner *Lusitania* is sunk by German submarine.

1916—Wilson is reelected president.

1917—U.S. breaks diplomatic relations with Germany. Czar Nicholas of Russia abdicates as revolution begins. U.S. declares war on Austria-Hungary. John F. Kennedy is born in Brookline, Massachusetts.

1918—Wilson proclaims "Fourteen Points" as war aims. On November 11, armistice is signed between Allies and Germany.

1919—Eighteenth Amendment prohibits sale and manufacture of intoxicating liquors. Wilson presides over first League of Nations; wins Nobel Peace Prize. Theodore Roosevelt dies in Oyster Bay, New York.

1920—Nineteenth Amendment (women's suffrage) is passed. Warren Harding is elected president.

1921—Adolf Hitler's stormtroopers begin to terrorize political opponents.

1922—Irish Free State is established. Soviet states form USSR. Benito Mussolini forms Fascist government in Italy.

1923—President Harding dies in San Francisco, California; he is succeeded by Vice-President Calvin Coolidge.

1924—Coolidge is elected president. Woodrow Wilson dies in Washington, D.C. James Carter is born in Plains, Georgia. George Bush is born in Milton, Massachusetts.

1925—Hitler reorganizes Nazi Party and publishes first volume of *Mein Kampf.*

1926—Fascist youth organizations founded in Germany and Italy. Republic of Lebanon proclaimed.

1927—Stalin becomes Soviet dictator. Economic conference in Geneva attended by fifty-two nations.

1928—Herbert Hoover is elected president. U.S. and many other nations sign Kellogg-Briand pacts to outlaw war.

1929—Stock prices in New York crash on "Black Thursday"; the Great Depression begins.

1930—Bank of U.S. and its many branches close (most significant bank failure of the year). William Howard Taft dies in Washington, D.C.

1931—Emigration from U.S. exceeds immigration for first time as Depression deepens.

1932—Franklin D. Roosevelt wins presidential election in a Democratic landslide.

1933—First concentration camps are erected in Germany. U.S. recognizes USSR and resumes trade. Twenty-First Amendment repeals prohibition. Calvin Coolidge dies in Northampton, Massachusetts.

1934—Severe dust storms hit Plains states. President Roosevelt passes U.S. Social Security Act.

1936—Roosevelt is reelected. Spanish Civil War begins. Hitler and Mussolini form Rome-Berlin Axis.

1937—Roosevelt signs Neutrality Act.

1938—Roosevelt sends appeal to Hitler and Mussolini to settle European problems amicably.

1939—Germany takes over Czechoslovakia and invades Poland, starting World War II.

1940 — Roosevelt is reelected for a third term.

1941 — Japan bombs Pearl Harbor, U.S. declares war on Japan. Germany and Italy declare war on U.S.; U.S. then declares war on them.

1942 — Allies agree not to make separate peace treaties with the enemies. U.S. government transfers more than 100,000 Nisei (Japanese-Americans) from west coast to inland concentration camps.

1943 — Allied bombings of Germany begin.

1944 — Roosevelt is reelected for a fourth term. Allied forces invade Normandy on D-Day.

1945 — President Franklin D. Roosevelt dies in Warm Springs, Georgia; Vice-President Harry S. Truman succeeds him. Mussolini is killed; Hitler commits suicide. Germany surrenders. U.S. drops atomic bomb on Hiroshima; Japan surrenders: end of World War II.

1946 — U.N. General Assembly holds its first session in London. Peace conference of twenty-one nations is held in Paris.

1947 — Peace treaties are signed in Paris. "Cold War" is in full swing.

1948 — U.S. passes Marshall Plan Act, providing $17 billion in aid for Europe. U.S. recognizes new nation of Israel. India and Pakistan become free of British rule. Truman is elected president.

1949 — Republic of Eire is proclaimed in Dublin. Russia blocks land route access from Western Germany to Berlin; airlift begins. U.S., France, and Britain agree to merge their zones of occupation in West Germany. Apartheid program begins in South Africa.

1950 — Riots in Johannesburg, South Africa, against apartheid. North Korea invades South Korea. U.N. forces land in South Korea and recapture Seoul.

1951 — Twenty-Second Amendment limits president to two terms.

1952 — Dwight D. Eisenhower resigns as supreme commander in Europe and is elected president.

1953 — Stalin dies; struggle for power in Russia follows. Rosenbergs are executed for espionage.

1954 — U.S. and Japan sign mutual defense agreement.

1955 — Blacks in Montgomery, Alabama, boycott segregated bus lines.

1956 — Eisenhower is reelected president. Soviet troops march into Hungary.

1957 — U.S. agrees to withdraw ground forces from Japan. Russia launches first satellite, *Sputnik*.

1958 — European Common Market comes into being. Fidel Castro begins war against Batista government in Cuba.

1959 — Alaska becomes the forty-ninth state. Hawaii becomes fiftieth state. Castro becomes premier of Cuba. De Gaulle is proclaimed president of the Fifth Republic of France.

1960 — Historic debates between Senator John F. Kennedy and Vice-President Richard Nixon are televised. Kennedy is elected president. Brezhnev becomes president of USSR.

1961 — Berlin Wall is constructed. Kennedy and Khrushchev confer in Vienna. In Bay of Pigs incident, Cubans trained by CIA attempt to overthrow Castro.

1962 — U.S. military council is established in South Vietnam.

1963 — Riots and beatings by police and whites mark civil rights demonstrations in Birmingham, Alabama; 30,000 troops are called out, Martin Luther King, Jr., is arrested. Freedom marchers descend on Washington, D.C., to demonstrate. President Kennedy is assassinated in Dallas, Texas; Vice-President Lyndon B. Johnson is sworn in as president.

1964 — U.S. aircraft bomb North Vietnam. Johnson is elected president. Herbert Hoover dies in New York City.

1965 — U.S. combat troops arrive in South Vietnam.

1966 — Thousands protest U.S. policy in Vietnam. National Guard quells race riots in Chicago.

1967 — Six-Day War between Israel and Arab nations.

1968 — Martin Luther King, Jr., is assassinated in Memphis, Tennessee. Senator Robert Kennedy is assassinated in Los Angeles. Riots and police brutality take place at Democratic National Convention in Chicago. Richard Nixon is elected president. Czechoslovakia is invaded by Soviet troops.

1969—Dwight D. Eisenhower dies in Washington, D.C. Hundreds of thousands of people in several U.S. cities demonstrate against Vietnam War.

1970—Four Vietnam War protesters are killed by National Guardsmen at Kent State University in Ohio.

1971—Twenty-Sixth Amendment allows eighteen-year-olds to vote.

1972—Nixon visits Communist China; is reelected president in near-record landslide. Watergate affair begins when five men are arrested in the Watergate hotel complex in Washington, D.C. Nixon announces resignations of aides Haldeman, Ehrlichman, and Dean and Attorney General Kleindienst as a result of Watergate-related charges. Harry S. Truman dies in Kansas City, Missouri.

1973—Vice-President Spiro Agnew resigns; Gerald Ford is named vice-president. Vietnam peace treaty is formally approved after nineteen months of negotiations. Lyndon B. Johnson dies in San Antonio, Texas.

1974—As a result of Watergate cover-up, impeachment is considered; Nixon resigns and Ford becomes president. Ford pardons Nixon and grants limited amnesty to Vietnam War draft evaders and military deserters.

1975—U.S. civilians are evacuated from Saigon, South Vietnam, as Communist forces complete takeover of South Vietnam.

1976—U.S. celebrates its Bicentennial. James Earl Carter becomes president.

1977—Carter pardons most Vietnam draft evaders, numbering some 10,000.

1980—Ronald Reagan is elected president.

1981—President Reagan is shot in the chest in assassination attempt. Sandra Day O'Connor is appointed first woman justice of the Supreme Court.

1983—U.S. troops invade island of Grenada.

1984—Reagan is reelected president. Democratic candidate Walter Mondale's running mate, Geraldine Ferraro, is the first woman selected for vice-president by a major U.S. political party.

1985—Soviet Communist Party secretary Konstantin Chernenko dies; Mikhail Gorbachev succeeds him. U.S. and Soviet officials discuss arms control in Geneva. Reagan and Gorbachev hold summit conference in Geneva. Racial tensions accelerate in South Africa.

1986—Space shuttle *Challenger* explodes shortly after takeoff; crew of seven dies. U.S. bombs bases in Libya. Corazon Aquino defeats Ferdinand Marcos in Philippine presidential election.

1987—Iraqi missile rips the U.S. frigate *Stark* in the Persian Gulf, killing thirty-seven American sailors. Congress holds hearings to investigate sale of U.S. arms to Iran to finance Nicaraguan *contra* movement.

1988—President Reagan and Soviet leader Gorbachev sign INF treaty, eliminating intermediate nuclear forces. Severe drought sweeps the United States. George Bush is elected president.

1989—East Germany opens Berlin Wall, allowing citizens free exit. Communists lose control of governments in Poland, Romania, and Czechoslovakia. Chinese troops massacre over 1,000 pro-democracy student demonstrators in Beijing's Tiananmen Square.

1990—Iraq annexes Kuwait, provoking the threat of war. East and West Germany are reunited. The Cold War between the United States and the Soviet Union comes to a close. Several Soviet republics make moves toward independence.

1991—Backed by a coalition of members of the United Nations, U.S. troops drive Iraqis from Kuwait. Latvia, Lithuania, and Estonia withdraw from the USSR. The Soviet Union dissolves as its republics secede to form a Commonwealth of Independent States.

1992—U.N. forces fail to stop fighting in territories of former Yugoslavia. More than fifty people are killed and more than six hundred buildings burned in rioting in Los Angeles. U.S. unemployment reaches eight-year high. Hurricane Andrew devastates southern Florida and parts of Louisiana. International relief supplies and troops are sent to combat famine and violence in Somalia.

1993—U.S.-led forces use airplanes and missiles to attack military targets in Iraq. William Jefferson Clinton becomes the forty-second U.S. president.

1994—Richard M. Nixon dies in New York City.

Index

Page numbers in boldface type indicate illustrations.

About the Author

Jim Hargrove has worked as a writer and editor for more than ten years. After serving as an editorial director for three Chicago area publishers, he began a career as an independent writer, preparing a series of books for children. He has contributed to works by nearly twenty different publishers. His Childrens Press titles include biographies of Mark Twain and Richard Nixon. With his wife and daughter, he lives in a small Illinois town near the Wisconsin border.